Nolan,

Granny Sue Sue H
enjoy reading about

MW01355098

Please enjoy,

Tiffany Bryant

TWO STORIES ABOUT TEDDY THE CHEF

Copyright © 2022 Tiffany Bryant
All rights reserved
First Edition

PAGE PUBLISHING
Conneaut Lake, PA

First originally published by Page Publishing 2022

ISBN 978-1-6624-8519-0 (hc)
ISBN 978-1-6624-8518-3 (digital)

Printed in the United States of America

ADOPTION DAY

Hello, my name is Teddy, and I am a black-and-white cocker spaniel poodle mix puppy, and I am sad. Since cooking is the one activity that cheers me up, I'm hanging out in the kitchen today searching for the ingredients to make my famous pumpkin treats.

I quickly gathered up and mixed one can of pumpkin, sugar, all-purpose flour, vanilla, cinnamon, and a few eggs to make my younger golden-haired sister Sammy some pumpkin treats to take with her on her long car ride to her forever home. I'm sad because when she leaves I will be the only puppy left at the foster home.

While I was taking the pumpkin treats out of the oven, I heard the van taking Sammy away pull up the driveway. I looked out the kitchen window and was surprised to see a younger blonde teenage girl get out of the van with the older woman who was adopting Sammy.

I quickly wrapped up the pumpkin treats and took them to the living room.

When I arrived in the living room, the teenage girl named Nina couldn't keep her eyes off of me, and she started talking to my foster parents about me and if I had a forever home too. When they told her I was the last littermate to be adopted, she began telling the older woman named Grandma about how it would be nice for Sammy to have her brother as a companion and that she should adopt me too.

I couldn't believe what I was hearing, so I whispered in Sammy's ear to find out if what I had heard about adopting me, too, was for real. Sammy assured me it was as she gave me a big hug. Yes, the older lady agreed with the teenage girl that adopting two littermates was a great idea.

The older lady began asking my foster parents if I could be adopted too. They assured her that yes she could adopt me along with Sammy.

Then my foster parents helped me pack my kitchen supplies and clothes so I could join Sammy in the van for our departure to our new forever home.

NEW HOME

• • • • • • • • • • • •

As the van pulled up the circular driveway and stopped outside a large red brick house, Grandma asked Nina to take Teddy and Sammy into the house and show us our rooms in our new home.

When we entered the grand hall, a rather tall man who Nina called Grandpa greeted us at the door. Grandpa bent down and picked Sammy up; he couldn't believe how beautiful my sister was. Then the tall man, named Grandpa asked Nina who I was, and she told him the story of how my name was Teddy, and I was Sammy's littermate.

About that time Grandma entered the grand hall, and she added how fabulous my pumpkin treats were and that I would be helping her in the kitchen prepare meals for everyone in the house.

After introductions Nina continued to show Sammy and me our new bedrooms, and we were told to unpack our things, relax, and meet everyone in the dining room at 7:00 p.m. for supper.

As I was talking to Sammy about our new home and how excited I was to be able to help in the kitchen I began to smell onions, and I knew I had to rush to the kitchen to see if I could help Grandma prepare the supper.

I began to follow the onion smell to the kitchen. I noticed that no one was in the kitchen and the onions needed to be stirred soon before they began burning. I grabbed a spoon and turned down the heat. As I surveyed the countertops I noticed ingredients that would create a fabulous spaghetti sauce. I decided to add the hamburger meat to the onions as well as some fresh garlic and a little salt and pepper. Once the hamburger had browned I began opening cabinets looking for a colander to drain the oil from the browned meat. About that time, Grandma entered the kitchen, and she smiled real big. She was so happy that I had taken over while she had stepped away, and we began to prepare the spaghetti sauce.

We added the crushed tomatoes to the browned meat, and I picked some fresh basil from Grandma's herb box above the window sill and added it to the sauce.

While the pasta sauce simmered Grandma made the pasta while I created a salad and placed the garlic bread in the oven to add to our meal.

Once the sauce, pasta, and bread were done I helped Grandma take the food into the dining room. While we all sat down to eat my eyes glanced at Sammy, and we smiled at each other because we knew we would enjoy living with Grandma and Grandpa.

ABOUT THE AUTHOR

I am an Arizona State University alumni. Due to COVID and the fact that I was diagnosed with multiple sclerosis twenty-five years ago I recently retired as a Special Education Teacher. I currently reside in Deep East Texas where I live on a small ranchette surrounded by animals and a small garden. I married late in life and my stepchildren have blessed my husband with three grandsons and sometimes I am called Nana.

CPSIA information can be obtained
at www.ICGtesting.com
Printed in the USA
JSHW022252181022
31851JS00002B/10